Furious Frank

This book is all about Frank.
Frank is a chameleon that struggles controlling strong emotions,
but particularly his anger.

The methods Frank uses in this book have come from research with
organisations intrinsic to neurodiversity.

ADHD UK
www.adhduk.co.uk

National Autistic Society
www.autism.org.uk

In addition to the UK's National Health Service (NHS).

Mind, the mental health charity.
When you're thinking about your own mental health, or someone else's,
having access to the right information is vital. Visit our website at
www.mind.org.uk

There are a variety of techniques available when it comes to
management of big feelings and emotions.
If it becomes a concern, it is always recommended
to speak to your GP.

This Is...

Frank.

Frank

is

Awesome.

He loves to read, and can be buried in his favourite book for ages.

He paints
beautiful
works of art.

He loves playing

FOOTBALL

Though he hasn't quite figured out how to make the ball move properly.

He is the master of

HIDE

and

SEEK

But sometimes...

Frank

can become

FURIOUS FRANK.

He can get frustrated while
playing his games.

There are even times where Frank
doesn't know why,
he just starts to feel so
FURIOUS!

His friends and family ask him to calm down,
but he just

EXPLODES.

He starts shouting and
is mean to the people he cares about.

Frank's parents also become frustrated.

They struggle to calm him down and
end up having to tell him off.

This does

NOT

help Frank's fury.

Not at all.

And Frank gets sent to

his room,

and his toys get
taken away.

After a while,
Frank begins to calm down.

He remembers some of the mean things he has said.

He becomes anxious and sad.

He starts to worry that no one will like him
any more.

Frank needs to

APOLOGISE

for what FURIOUS FRANK has said.

Frank's parents decide to do some

RESEARCH

They want to teach Frank
how to control his fury.

They are worried about FURIOUS FRANK.

They take Frank to see Doctor Hugo.

He is lovely and kind.
He asks Frank about what he enjoys,
what makes him happy,
and all about **FURIOUS FRANK**.

Dr Hugo tells Frank that *sometimes* it
can be really hard to control your emotions..

But he has some tips and tricks to help him
manage his emotions!

Can you do them too?

He tells him to take one finger and follow the outline of his other hand.

BREATHE IN

for the red lines...

And

BREATHE OUT

for the blue lines.

CUDDLE
A TEDDY

or

FIDGET with
A
SPINNER!

Talk out loud and list..

FIVE

Things you can **see**.

FOUR

Things you can **touch**.

THREE

Things you can **hear**.

TWO

Things you can **smell**.

ONE

Things you can **taste**.

Or you can

LISTEN TO MUSIC!

(You can even sing along, if you want to!)

Sometimes the best thing you can do is

**TAKE YOURSELF
AWAY**.

Have a bit of alone time to relax.
Maybe a little nap, or just have a lie down.

Or try one of your other hobbies!

Do something that makes you smile!

Frank couldn't wait to try them out!
And so, the next time Frank started to feel overwhelmed...

He put his hand out in front of him..

And started taking tracing his finger
up and down the fingers on his other hand,
taking
DEEP BREATHS
IN and **OUT**

The first time he did this, he felt
A LITTLE BETTER..

Then the second time..
A BIT BETTER..

Then finally..

IT WORKED!

Frank started to feel like
himself again!

Little by little, he learned when he was losing control…

And by taking one step at a time, he was able to feel better.

Get Away

Breathe

Draw

Calm

...It didn't ALWAYS work.

Every so often, Frank's emotions would be
so strong that no matter what he tried, he still

EXPLODED

...And that's OK.

Because Frank knew that the tips and tricks were helping.

He was still learning how to control his emotions.

Even grown ups get **FURIOUS** sometimes.

Frank started TALKING to his family about his emotions
and realised they were always going to be there
to give him

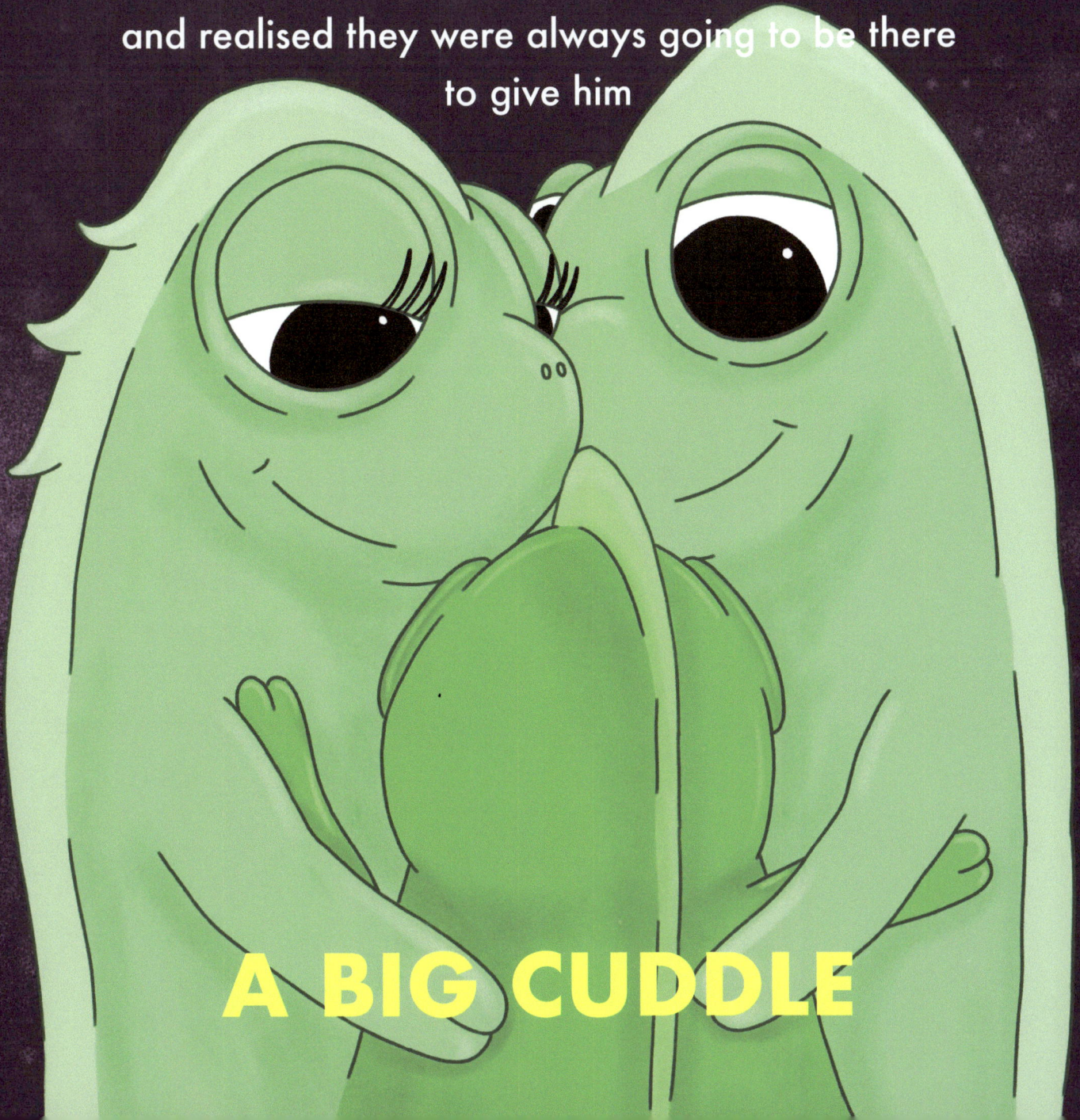

A BIG CUDDLE

But...

MOST OF THE TIME

it really helped.

Frank started to feel much more

CALM AND RELAXED.

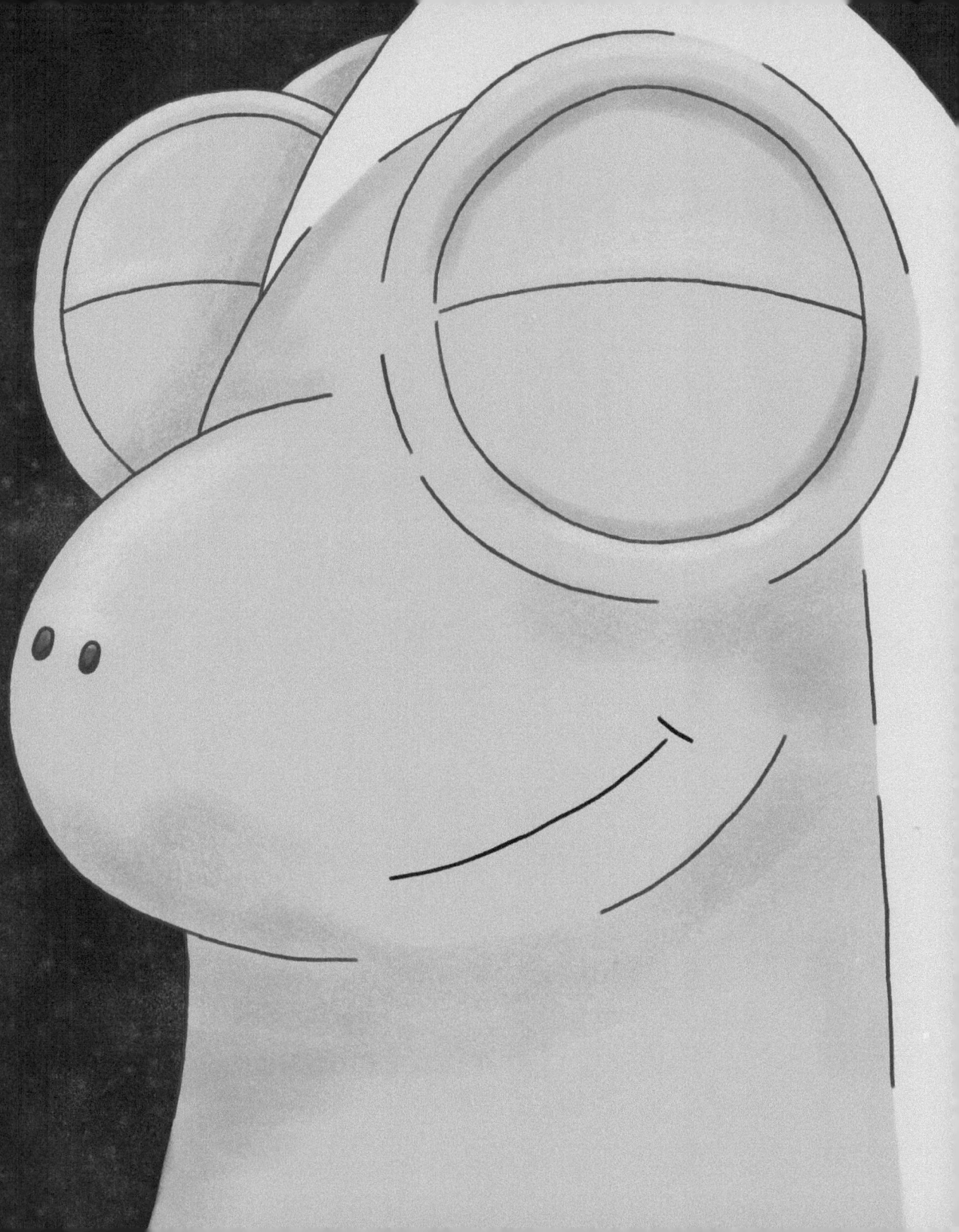

Frank decided he also wanted to write his own

JOURNAL!

Maybe if he writes down **HOW**

he feels, and **WHY**,

then he can
find out exactly what triggers
FURIOUS FRANK.

But that's for Frank's eyes only.

Frank is much happier now that
he's learned how to

CALM HIMSELF DOWN

and

MANAGE HIS FEELINGS.

And

FURIOUS FRANK

is not a
problem any more!

Well...

MOST OF
THE TIME

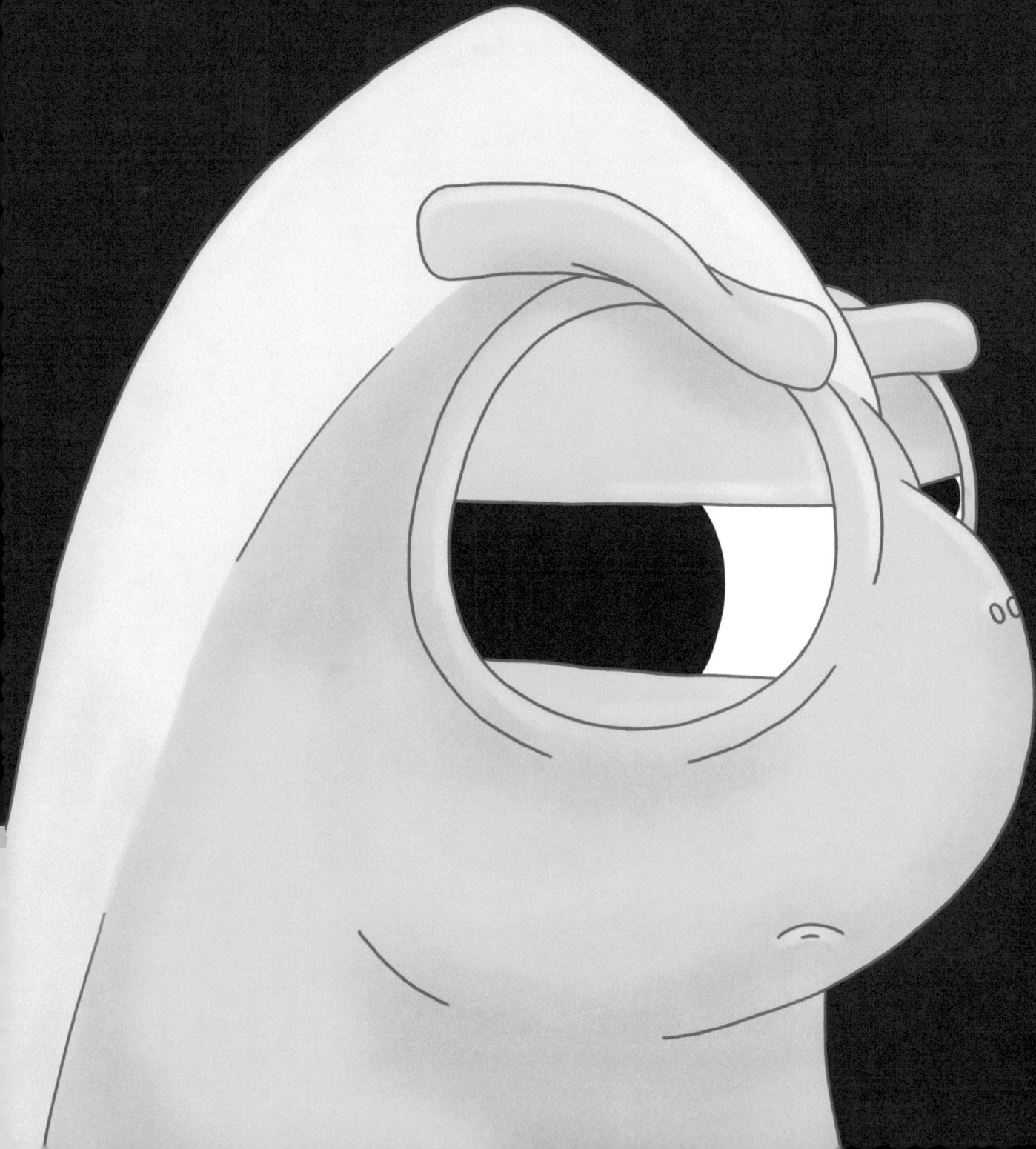

Need More Help?

This book is designed to help children find ways to cope with their own powerful emotions that can, at times, become overwhelming.

This could be for any number of reasons, some are more complex to solve than others, but help is out there.

FURIOUS FRANK

www.ingramcontent.com/pod-product-compliance
Lightning Source LLC
LaVergne TN
LVHW072107070426
835509LV00002B/58